tell the fireflies i'm sorry

eliza grant

Paperback: 978-0-578-37419-2
Ebook: 978-0-578-37418-5

for every firefly i ever caught. fly free, little one.

From my rotting body, flowers will grow,
and I am in them and that is eternity.

— Edvard Munch

i'll watch your life in pictures
(inspired by *Last Kiss* by Taylor Swift)

do you know what hurts
even more than the leaving?
it's the hand-me-down knowledge
of the ways you're changing,
the photographed smiles
i can no longer decipher.
i hate this one-way mirror
that i watch you through,
made of pictures and rumors
and secondhand stories.
there was a time when i could swear
our souls had sprouted from the same soil,
and our brains swam among the same stars.
there was a time when i didn't have to try
to know you, because to know you
was to know myself.
i don't think i know either of us anymore.
but still, i'll toss aside my pride
and beg your friends for a tale or two
about how you've been,
and what you're doing,
and if you're happy.
there was a time when we swore
we'd grow old together,
but i don't think we realized then
that we weren't even finished growing up.

1

i hate that i don't get to know
the person you're becoming.
i hate that i'm not the same person
you loved.

leave a message at the tone

sorry i missed your call.
i've been busy
tying to outrun
my shadow.
i've just got a lot on my plate
these days, like soul-patching
and brain-freezing
and sleep-sinking.
i'll call you back
once i figure out
how to untwist the thoughts
that have herded in my head
like a throng of blood-hungry hornets.
i'll call you back
once i manage to lose
my shadow.

the treehouse

royal blue midnight poured
through the wooden window
like a wineglass full of watercolors.
somewhere deep inside the trunk of the old oak
we heard a family of owls cooing each other
to sleep. the floorboards creaked
but did not falter. every time
we'd laugh too hard, that riotous,
hyena-cub sort of laughter, the kind
that seems to shake the very solar system,
we thought the planks would give way
underneath us.
instead they only shifted,
absorbing our weight,
welcoming us as an extension
of an extension,
of the tree.

the child-of-divorce's revolt

for lips that crack
for pride and blame
for patchwork skin that bleeds the same
for the ties that bind me to your name
i'll burn our kingdom down

for school bus blues
for coffee spilt
for flower girls and brides that wilt
for tilt-a-whirls that never tilt
i'll burn our kingdom down

for picket-fenced
suburban lies
for christmas cards with hollow eyes
for fights patrolled by stairwell spies
i'll burn our kingdom down

for whiskey oaths
for vows that stall
for homespun hell down every hall
for leaps of faith that hit a wall
i'll burn our kingdom down

for cutting loose
a losing game
for guilty hearts that break the same

for fires lit by lonesome flames
i'll burn our kingdom down

for the ties that bind me to your name
i'll burn our kingdom down.

double negatives

my calculus teacher says math and life
are the same, but math tells us
that all double negatives will inevitably
cancel each other out and, like alchemy,
conjure up a positive. life tells us
that it doesn't care how many contradictions
are stacked on top of each other—
there can always be another un-negated
negative. another injustice. another outrage.

i'd like to think you and i are the anomaly.
maybe we're life's only true double negative,
us two skeptics with our charred hearts.
and maybe, maybe, maybe,
we will cancel each other out.

imaginary

when i was young i knew a girl
made out of refracted light.
she emerged when the dawn
hit the dust particles just so,
a playmate-shaped halo,
a sun-streaked blaze. together,
hand in ghostly hand,
we danced through worlds
far kinder than this one.
which one of us was made of myth,
and which of heart and hope?
the boundary grew as misty
as her sweet silhouette.

i haven't seen my iridescent friend
in quite some time now. oftentimes
i wonder if she was more honest,
even as a fragment of fiction,
than anyone i know today.
perhaps realness is not qualified
by the pulsing of a heart, but rather,
the ability to fill someone
with the sense
that they are seen.

distance

where will this moment (this band-aid
of peace that i call forever and you call
a little while) go when it dies?

when you leave me,
as we both know you will
but pretend you won't,
where else will i find
company without the burden of noise?
closeness that does not require touch?
i contain enough chaos.
the whirlwinds of chemicals
that have been wreaking havoc
on my head these days
have all but worn me out.
i need someone to be still with. someone
who will sit beside me on the bed but leave
an inch of space between us.
hush little hurricane, close your eyes.
rest here 'til the riot dies.

inches turn to miles when the world keeps
spinning but my feet stay planted
in this familiar filth. we both know
that i'm too stubborn to revise my will,
my code of living and dying.
that inch of distance i require

is loaded with reasons
for all of my someones
to eventually run. that inch embodies
all of the fine print written on my forehead.
all of the warning labels
stamped across my skin.

descension

what if that brightness
we thought was a silver lining
is just the sun growing weaker,
wearier, sick
of holding herself up?
what if she's begun
to droop down
towards the earth?
towards us?

is it terrible
that i wouldn't blame her
if she dropped?

four billion years is a long time
to linger. i've had trouble
not nose-diving
in just these nineteen.

feelings that don't have names

1. catching the eye of a stranger who looks to be about your age in an airport, especially when it's early morning and the clouds are as fragile and flushed as spun sugar and the sun is still low in the sky. it feels like love, a little bit, the way you stare at each other, but the sort of love that was never meant to stretch beyond a single moment. your twin gazes whisper, *i have never spoken to you, never learned your name or your favorite song or the words you murmur in your sleep, but i think i have fallen in love with you, even knowing i will never see you again.*

2. the night before a birthday.

3. tee-shirt weather in december.

4. standing half-hunched over the sink in a bathroom at a party, when the music outside sounds as if it's coming from underwater, and you're half-drunk and half-sad and half-euphoric. all the porcelain is a blinding white, so white that it hurts your teeth, and you look into the mirror and gawk at yourself, thinking, *so this is who i'm always going to be.*

5. eleventh birthdays. staying up until midnight but never getting your hogwarts letter.

* * *

6. idolizing dead people.

7. children playing war. watching them sword-fight with hockey sticks and load rifles made from cardboard. watching them mimic death, watching them to their knees and groan before going terribly, chillingly still. watching them pop back up a few seconds later, laughing with their pretend-murderer.

8. realizing that you've outgrown that sort of smiling-so-big-it-hurts enthusiasm.

9. waking up in a cold sweat. knowing you had a nightmare but not being able to remember what it was about.

10. a "see you later" that never came true.

three, two, one

the year is almost over
and we are going under with it.
this was always how it was going to end,
and yet it seems absurd
that the firework we nurtured
has finally fizzled out.
this countdown is a callous thing.
it has made us begin
to miss each other
before we've even left.

save it

move the pill bottles off of the counter,
you say. *keep them out of my sight.*

the tornado-heads of the world
are too turbulent for your clear skies
so we're both pretending
i'm not one of them.

you'll choose not to notice
when i'm cheek to cheek
with the bathroom floor,
and i'll choose to shelter you

from the remnants of wreckage past
tempests have left below my skull.
you say we should shelve away
my demons but, if you're not careful,

soon you're going to meet them.
tell me one more time to *calm down*
while i'm drowning
and i will drag you under.

this life vest you've thrown me
feels more like an anchor,
but maybe that's just me.
maybe i'm the paperweight

15

* * *

tied to your balloon string.
maybe some people
are destined to float above it all,

and others were doomed from birth
to someday sink.

random word generator poem #1: gem, myth, viable, parachute

perhaps there are rare gems nestled
inside the stones they threw at me.
for sanity's sake, i will not break
them open. shelving the maybe-jewels,
maybe-ammunition is always
a viable option. the alchemist never fails
if she never sticks around to watch
the copper mature into gold, so
fasten the wool around my eyes.
secure it with cement. i will see
only softness. immerse me in myths
of the craftsman and his son,
of labyrinths and legends, of feathers
and wax. but when the little boy
with the fragile wings is blinded
by the ecstasy of the salt-scented air,
when he cannot resist the splendor
of the sun, write me a new ending.
convince me that Icarus
was wearing a parachute.

bathroom pack

we knew just by the murmuring
that the boys were full of wonder.
they wondered why us girls
always went to the bathroom in packs,
and they wondered about the secrets
that lay cushioned beneath our curves,
shielded in our satin stretch marks,
and they wondered how we moved
like a desert dust storm
made from hourglass sand.

we did not wonder. we knew
all we wished to know.
we shut ourselves inside
and reveled in our friendship.
every second we wasted
calming our tissue paper souls
atop the bathroom floor
was a quiet sort of lovely.

never have i ever

you and i survived on double-dares
and reckless abandon.

my mother always says
it was a miracle that we didn't die

trying to impress each other.
what she doesn't say,

the subtext that sways
in the air above me like a neon sign

hung by a noose,
is that we almost did. you and i

were almost swallowed
by the siren song of danger,

the dark-hearted allure of pain,
the devilish draw of dipping our toes

into the void just to prove
that we were brave enough

to look fate in the face
and ask it to fuck with us. with us,

* * *

it was always a game
of who could climb higher,

who could deprive themself for longer,
who was more willing to peer

over the edge and discover what lay
on the bottom of the canyon.

we lived life wobbling on a tightrope,
always tempting each other to lift up

one foot. i don't think either of us
knew we were capable of plummeting

to the ground until one of us did.
before then, we were too distracted by life

to believe in such trivial things
as death.

don't let anyone tell you otherwise

i hope you know
what an extraordinary feat it is
to remain rooted to the ground
even when the thunderclouds
are begging you to float away
and join them. even when the very sky
seems to beckon you upwards.
you are brave for staying today.
do not forget that.

alternate realities

i saw an old couple walking arm in arm
in matching sweaters, sea-foam green,
and i thought that perhaps
they were an alternate version of us,
in a gentler lifetime than this one.
and it aches, how clearly i could picture it;
the two of them (the two of us)
slow-dancing to Sinatra
in the brothy kitchen light at 2am.
red wine on the counter,
twilight in their eyes,
swaying past picture frames
populated by grandchildren
and trips to the lake. and at some point,
his forehead (your forehead) would fall
against hers (mine), and they'd stay
fused together as they waltzed,
their heartbeats in their heads,
their twin skulls whispering
a secret language of cerebral certainty:
you are the only one I would do this with.
you are the only one.

the art of falling apart

i once believed that strength
only came in disciplined tear ducts.
eyes that knew never to water.
i thought that to cry
was to show my cards, reveal
the frightened child still stuck
on the tip of my tongue.
but the clouds never held in their rain
for fear of the sun's judgement—
they let their tears fall without shame,
without the smothering of senses
we call willpower, and they knew
that when their sorrow drenched the earth,
it would eventually be sucked into the soil,
a sprinkling of sparks for new growth.
new roots, new vines, new lilacs,
new lessons. lessons in how to hurt loudly,
because you don't have to be unbreakable
to be strong. misery will always win
if you keep declaring war on it.
neither your head nor your heart
will be any weaker
by calling a cease-fire.

when we were wild

do you miss the untamed days like i do?
back when our laws
were made of sidewalk chalk?
back when forest tea parties,
us wild children barefoot
among the nightshade and thistle,
were the closest we came to civility?
do you remember the silhouettes
of your imaginary friends? can you still
trace their outlines in your mind as easily
as you can write your own name?
i wonder, can you still talk to them?
discuss your day, discuss the daisies
that the two of you used to tuck
behind each other's ears?
do you miss the untamed days like i do?
do you miss the slack-jawed reverence
we had for every corner of this world
back when magic didn't seem
quite so far
out of reach?

speck

today i am fresh out of loveliness.
i contain no turns of phrases
that run and flood and flow
from my fingertips like quicksilver.
someone confiscate my brain.
hypnotize me, switch me off.
i can't wrap my head around
my head, this cesspool
of cinders and cells.

today none of my nightmares
dissolved with the daylight
and i am filled with hatred
for this world that is so damned
by impermanence. today i refuse
to swallow the fact that every
beautiful thing will someday be
a beautiful thing of the past.

today my words feel like blood
on the page and i can't go outside
because i know the sun will be hanging
there, sneering down at me,
and it'll be the same fucking sun
as yesterday, because the sun pays
no mind to the tragedies of a speck like me.
today i am a speck.

today i am a dead matchstick.

gifted

there is the rose-colored illusion
and then there is the truth.
in the fantastical version, i'm the high-flier.
the headline. one of the whiz kids
who clawed and scratched their way up
the sides of the pit that they were stalled in.
a bounce-back burnout who can tell stories
of redemption and have that be enough.
someone who knows how to find salvation
in reality, who doesn't need to believe
that the universe has intentions
and grand plans
and a detailed map made just for me.

but the truth is this black hole
that i've found solace in is one
of my own design.
brick by treacherous brick,
i built this tomb.
the truth is that i am my own undertaker.
the truth is that when you've eclipsed
exhaustion, when you're so tired
you forget your name,
a bed of nails will do just fine.
the truth is that i'll lie here beside
the other washed-up wunderkinds
without a word of protest. the truth

is that there are millions of golden children,
but very few lustrous adults.
the truth, it seems,
is that when your grownup teeth grow in,
your rarity wears out.

letting go

if you decide that you must go
move mountains in the life
next door to this one, i'll be there
to hold your hand as you slip away.
please know that if i could
come with you, we'd be walking
arm in arm into the stars by now.
but you must leave and i must stay,
so all i can do is wave at you
from the other side of the window
as you set off to discover that better place
the others always talk about.
make sure you remember to come back
and say hello once in a while.
i'll look for you in every bolt
of lightning, every shard of sea glass,
every gold-beaked hummingbird.
perhaps if i reach deep enough
into the horizon,
our hands will intertwine
once more.

fool's gold

for centuries, pyrite
has been hoodwinking miners
with its false luster,
it's counterfeit dignity.
fool's gold, they call it, but only after
they've been fooled.
the masquerade ends
the second someone bites
into the stone.
real gold remains unbroken.
pyrite, like a firework
of cheap dust,
shatters.

i don't let anyone get close
enough to bite into me.
i would surely crumble
underneath the jaws
of intimacy, and they'd realize
that radiance is no more
than a skin i occasionally step into.
they'd realize
what they thought was gold
is a knifelike shard
of pyrite.

the age of bulletproof backpacks

it's always the same.
every time a man with a gun strolls
into a school, the reporters search for glory
in the bloodshed. we call the slain children
fallen heroes, as if they signed on for being shot
when they enrolled in kindergarten.
as if they enlisted in an academic army
simply by stepping onto the school bus.
the fearless fighters of sandy hook, they say.
the noble warriors of parkland.
we use this valiant vernacular
after ever massacre, because it's easier
to stomach. because it means
they died brave. it means we don't
have to imagine them crying for their mothers
or begging for their barely-begun lives.
we make them into a neat little platoon
of toy soldiers, all lined up in a row,
smiling and plastic and entirely willing
to die for their country,
their homeland of cafeterias and classrooms
and lockers and desks and algebra tests.
do not kid yourself.
we did not enlist for this.
we do not die brave.

points for effort

i know that we were never very good
at playing soulmates,
but no one seems to pay much mind
to how hard we tried.
if wishful thinking had wings,
you and i would
be on our way
to jupiter by now.

sunken people

here is what you do not understand:
there are no first place medals
for wasting away.
you don't get to lounge
in your romanticized rendition
of rock bottom for very long
before you either have to grit your teeth
and climb out of it, or the darkness
washes over you entirely. irreversibly.
there is nothing beautiful down there.
flowers cannot stand such hollow places.

here is what you do not understand:
there is nothing noble about painting
a pretty picture of implosion. nothing kind
about flashing smiles at the children
who are watching you swan-dive
down the rabbit hole. you aren't selling
them a lean little promised land,
a latchkey to all things lovely.
you're selling them a boneyard. a pit
of quicksand full of sunken people
who have lost sight
of what's worth dying for.

there are children watching.
tell them the truth.

tell them there is nothing beautiful down there.

predestined

the line between meant to be
and meant to burn
is often made only of false hope
and deserted dreams.
there is no destiny
quite as decisive
as a promise
that was never intended
to be kept.

falling into place

it is entirely possible
to fall in love piece by piece.
first, i loved the way
your cheeks tug up and your lips
curl down when you're trying
to swallow a smile. then came
the journal by the side of your bed
in which you record your dreams,
even the one where the whole world
turned to stone and just you and i
were left unfrozen.

i fell in love with the way you cursed
at that man on the street who told
his son to quit acting like a girl.
i fell in love with your sleep-babble,
your witch-cackle laugh, your quiet days,
your sleepless nights,
your one chipped tooth,
your name. the way you said mine.
said it like it was something holy,
something to hold on to.

all of these things, i loved
and yet i did not know that i loved you,
the whole you, until that night
when you said that you were grateful

for the moon. i asked you why,
and you said, *because it's always there.*
because it never gives up on us.
that was the last piece.
that was when i knew.

random word generator poem #2: picture, future, blade, adult

if we were to go back through
our art class archives nowadays,
as these crude imitations of adults
we've become, i think the pictures
we drew in our youth would give us
paper cuts. the crayon-made
prophecies we never quite fulfilled—
when i grow up i will be untouchable—
would carve out our hardened hearts,
don't you agree? back then, the future
was made of cotton candy clouds,
not these phantom balls of vapor
we know now. out-dated innocence
is a blade. a vandal. i am relieved
that these greying versions of us
cannot cross courses with our younger
selves. i'm sure we'd snip
their construction paper wings
to smithereens.

one-night love affair

let's be soulmates for a night.
let's run away from this party,
this blue light and champagne shimmer.
pull me upstairs, and let's forget
that we're strangers. let's be each other's
favorite person for a moonrise. tell me
your secrets but not your name.
let's build a bond that's meant to be
broken. blown out like a birthday candle.
let's pay tribute to all things temporary,
to the hourglasses that live between
our ribcages. speak your mind,
spill your guts, bare your soul.
someday this will all expire, so drift
into my psyche 'till the sun comes up.
let's pretend we aren't responsible
for such fragile things as bodies.
turn off the lights and let's be born again
as silhouette-people, reduce ourselves
to the shadows we cast upon the mattress.
come tomorrow, soul-stranger, i will
remember your secrets but not your name.
that will be enough.

tell the fireflies i'm sorry

small lessons we learn as children—
don't let them see you cry, and some foods
are good and some are bad, and laziness
is the bane of productivity, and if he hits you
it means he likes you, and don't snitch,
don't tattletale, not ever—
are, in many ways, damning.
but the one that has chased me
the furthest through the tunnels
of this unsolvable labyrinth
that we call growing up
is: *the most humane thing*
you can do for a firefly
is to poke holes in the lid
of the jar you catch it in.
i thought i was so charitable
to shove a toothpick through the tinfoil
cinched atop the mason jar
and its flickering captive.
so it's only natural that as i grew,
i became content with semi-suffocation
so long as i was offered
a few gulps of fresh air
every now and again.
and it's only natural that i thought
the people who fed me
oxygen through straws,

like a jar-bound firefly,
were saints for being so kind
as to even let me breathe.
the most humane thing
you can do for a firefly
is not to catch it
at all.

a toast to time

so let's raise a glass to photographs
and expiration dates.
let's plan out our own epitaphs,
burn down the halls of fame.
it's such a shame that we all die
but that's the nature of the game,
and if your heart drifts off to sleep,
my dear, i'll love you just the same.

we've only got our bodies to blame.

solitary flowers

do not let the world persuade you
that loneliness is a flower
growing out of a sidewalk crack,
braving the footsteps of far crueler
creatures all by itself, gulping in
ash-thickened air and cigarette smoke,
kept company by only the pigeons.

i have found that oftentimes,
loneliness occurs in a field
of bluebells shrouded in dew
and a sweet country breeze,
where every stem sways the same
and all of the flowers blur together
into one mass of sapphire,
each petal indistinct from its roots.
from its source.

the lonesome are often the most
surrounded. the contented are often
the most alone.

girlhood

girlhood is being awed by the magnificent pink of rosewater and bubblegum and pepto-bismol but quickly raising your chin and pretending to loathe the color. it's stretch marks and chipped nails and feeling yourself grow and praying that it stops. it's letting skinned knees bleed and talking to butterflies when no one is watching and dodging every sidewalk crack for fear of your mother's shattered vertebrae. it's catcalls before you're old enough to know what they are. it's train rides and crossed knees and earbuds that aren't playing any music. *such a pretty girl. the things i would do to you.* tune out the terror with soundless music. don't look him in the eyes. tuck your keys between you fingers and wait. it's house parties, flashing lights, red solo cups, tight dresses, the curve of a waist, the majesty of a dancing girl, swaying like silk, like liquid gold. it's knowing the answer but keeping your hand down. it's underwire and lace. smudged mascara and watermelon gum. the taste of prozac stuck to the back of your tongue. it's locking eyes with the girls on the missing person's posters. *bring her home* and *if you see her please call* and *they've found a body.* it's wondering which picture they'd choose for you.

in the quiet

in the quiet, when my bones are bare,
where prayer and pain collide,
there are ghosts who keep me company,
and they don't know how they died.

in the quiet, in this space junk sphere
i've come to call my mind,
the walls have ears and i have words
the real world couldn't define.

in the quiet, with my ceiling God
who listens but won't reply
i play russian roulette
with imaginary friends
who left without saying goodbye.

in the morning, in the lull of dawn
as the circadian ache restarts,
i emerge from the murk of the quiet
and patch back together my parts.

when the fire dies

the air has shed its dewy summer skin
and now it's just as dry and cold as it was
on the day we unstuck ourselves for good.
sore throats and cloud-breaths and nights
that creep in quick and quiet,
they all tug me back towards our days
of crushing leaves and leaving
footprints in the frosted mud
of the forest, like boot-shaped calling cards
that we were there. *we were there.*
and i wish i could remember it better
and i wish i could forget it altogether.
the cold feels so much colder without you
here to summon up some kindling. you and i
are only soot now. the carcass of a fire.
and our candle, once blazing,
has become a puddle of wax
made from the leftover legacy
of Icarus' wings. each day, without you,
i return to this forest and gather up
our ashes in my pockets.
and as i sift through our embers, i mourn
the two dreamers who loved so hard
they choked their own flame.

the last night

tonight, under the willow tree,
we will let the crickets do all the talking.
my forehead will whisper precious lies
to yours, and the moon will hum
its usual song, the one that no one
ever named, and the honeysuckle
will rustle and reach, but it will be quiet.
we'll tell our secrets to the stars.
spill our demons to the dusk.
the ruthless truth—*this is the last night*
—is neater left unsaid, i think.
but tomorrow, the sunlight will cast
jagged halos across every spiderweb,
and the grasshoppers will rouse
to the glow of a Midas-touched dawn,
and even knowing that the home we built
has collapsed under the weight of itself,
you'll still whistle a backwards lullaby
and sing me awake.

an easy pill to swallow, a hard one to spit out

i can still feel your name lodged
in the back of my throat
like a half-swallowed pill.
you are the medicine
and you are the disease
and you are the child-lock
on the little orange bottle.
i suppose that makes me the child
with empty, eager hands who likes
to suck on the sugar
that coats your malignant capsules.
i am the child
who will pry away the plug of the poison
and gulp down your hate
like shrapnel syrup.

false front

the ship is going down
and the band is playing music.

i will slip below the ink-spill sea
with a smile on my face, and no one
will know that i'm sinking until
i've sunk, until the skeleton
of my scaffolding has been safely
tucked into salt-water grave.

the violin will trill
until the ocean soaks its strings.
the saxophone will warble
until it fills with brine.
the piano will chime
until it must gurgle goodbye.

as i go under, as i am swamped
by the undertow of life,
i will pantomime fineness.
the breach in my walls
where the water is rushing in
will be perfectly concealed
by the delicate melodies
drifting from the upper deck.
the band will croon on
until the very last note.

the very last breath.

the backslide

i can feel it starting again. the shaking. the slipping.
the ice growing thinner beneath me. that old friend, that
unwelcome visitor, that fungus in my brain. it has
begun to awaken. reawaken. i can feel it remembering
how to eat me alive. i thought i had a head full of
dormant monsters but maybe i just have a head full of
monsters who were resting for a little while. it's quite
unkind, don't you think, that i know what comes next? i
know exactly how the sickness will spread across my
skin, sprout like an overgrowth of poison ivy, squeezing
me, strangling me, coiling my body with vines. i know
exactly how the fungus will contaminate my
bloodstream, how it will corrupt and corrupt and
corrupt until it grows a heartbeat of its own. this is the
rumbling period. the half-quiet hush while the sinkhole
prepares itself to surface and split and swallow
everything in its path. and like i always do, i'll grow
weary. the monsters will suck me of my will. and soon,
upon the ice, the paper thin ice,
    i will sit
    and i will sleep.

the world is still spinning and i wish it would stop

these days, i can't stand the sound
of strangers laughing. i hate the way
the sun still glistens down
on morning dewdrops,
because how dare anything glisten?
how dare beauty carry on
like it hasn't been stripped
of its most precious possession—you?
normalcy leaves a bitter taste in my mouth,
a wretched weight in my lungs.
i consider everything that didn't implode
the very second you drifted away
to be cruel. i hate the birds for singing.
i hate the sun for rising. i hate
that the rest of the world hasn't flinched.
hasn't hurt. how can the sky be so okay?
how can the clouds still bear to float
when you're not here
for them to gaze down at?
these days, i can't stand anything
but the dark. i especially can't stand
that life goes on
without you.

keys

us girls become wolverines at night
when we slip our keys between our fingers.
when i get snatched, whenever it may be,
my fists will be saw-toothed. barbed
by female hysteria. i will go down
scratching, but i will still go down.
my cautions will sigh; *i told you so.*
my cautions and i know the rules
as lawfully as we know the statistics.
at least one in five women will be—
say *if*, i dare you.
in school we learn optimism
is the bane of diligence.
as rosy-cheeked fourth graders,
we're taught how to land a proper kick
to the groin. flat footed, with strength
in the heel. fifth grade is eye-pokes,
sixth is the punching techniques
that won't snap our wrists,
eighth is yelling *no* over and over again
at the men who are playing the roles
of the men who want us dead
or violated
or both.
tenth is where to buy mace.
i can't help but think
they're slowly giving up on us

not being snatched in the first place.
all i can do these days is tuck my keys
between my fingers and pray
that paranoia equates to protection. pray
that the nighttime figures want only a
smile, pretty girl. smile.

addendum to *keys:* not all men

not all men
snatch girls. i know that.
i also know that not all sharks
are inclined to nibble
on swimmer's legs.
if you want to get technical,
there are exponentially
more innocent sharks
than innocent men,
but still, we'll swim away,
and still, we'll slip
our locksmith's claws into place
when the nighttime figures
come creeping up behind us.
and still,
we'll do whatever it takes
to keep ourselves
from being bitten.

ghost

haunt me, if you must.
i'd rather be tortured by your memory
than smothered by amnesia.
if it's true this love has slipped
six feet underground, let it
come back and loom over me
like a specter on my shoulder.
let it linger, let it hurt,
let it drive me mad.
be my favorite poltergeist.
i'd rather run from you
in my nightmares
than not dream of you
at all.

seedling song

every flower that i've tried to love has died
feel their petals turn to dust
beneath my hand
my windowsill's a slaughterhouse,
my brain's a swarm of bees
chasing nectar on this dry and barren land

maybe growth is just a game that people play
when change feels like a chain
around their necks
maybe springtime is a sham,
maybe flowers only bloom
because that's what all the gardeners expect.

Garlic City

Snapple Fact #265:
90% of all garlic consumed in the US
comes from Gilroy, California.
Doesn't that just reek of integrity?
Can't you picture a city
made entirely of garlic,
heads upon heads forged
into pungent skyscrapers,
clove-people pushing their seedlings
around in strollers
made from papery garlic skin,
showing off their acrid little bundles of joy
to passerby vegetables?
I wonder if there's some garlic-y magic
to Gilroy or if it's just another city
like this one, only with fouler breath.
How, then, is the world such a place
that there was a shooting
at the Gilroy Garlic Festival?
It was four years ago, the 41st annual,
because nothing can be so perfect
as a city that simply adores garlic.
And I'll fumble for the words to say
that his AR-15 was a snuffer,
and the purity of their being such thing
as a garlic festival
was an open flame.

Or perhaps his gun was a matchstick.
Does that sound more poetic?
Maybe Gilroy was a paper house.
"Why are you doing this?"
someone in the crowd yelled at the shooter.
"Because I'm really angry," he replied.
Three people were killed,
ages 6, 13, and 25. At a garlic festival.
Because he was really angry.
There is nothing beautiful there,
not in the baby-toothed
smile of Stephen Romero
standing hand and hand
with his grandmother
beneath an inflatable man
with a head of garlic
for a head. Not in the balmy breeze
that brought about the smell of fried food
smothered in earthy garlic and hot butter.
Not in the way that he giggled,
the sound itself like homegrown youth,
or in the way he outstretched his tiny arm
towards the Garlic Ice Cream booth,
or in the way he blazed across the grass
like a flicker-boy, a firefly,
towards the wire fence
that would, five minutes later,
be torn through with an angry man's
bolt cutters. Not even in the particular blue

of the July sky.
There are limits to what poetry can impart.
There are lines that stretch
beyond the threshold of words.
Some people get to grow up,
and some are like Stephen Romero,
and there aren't any metaphors
that can possibly explain why that is.

you are so remembered down here

i often think about the fact that,
in the middle ages, some believed
that the dead could sense it each time
someone on earth remembered them.
i imagine the fumes of my nostalgia
reaching you in the tinkling
of wind chimes, like the ones
you used to run your fingers through.
remember how the brass rods danced
in the daybreak? how we watched them
shine like sacred suns?

i'm not yet certain if i'm unscathed enough
to believe in such beautiful things
as an afterlife, but if those olden folk
got it right, if the memories can seep
from my skull and into your spirit,
i hope each time you hear that chiming,
you feel me reaching across the cosmos,
scouring the sky
for one more trace of your scent,
one more flicker of your smile.

old friends `

we knew, of course, that our youth
was nothing more than a glass house.
a wide-eyed wonder that existed to end.

the monkey bar calluses have peeled away,
the scraped knees long since healed.

do you remember when recklessness
was our only constitution?
when we could blame
every mistake on our
not-quite-developed brains?

your faces are photographs
and the ink is fading.

there's a boundlessness buried
in the memories i am beginning to forget,
and i fear i'll never reach it,

or you,
again.

briefly everlasting

what if the great beyond was here on earth?
what if Eden was really
your grandmother's garden in June,
when the air smelled of honeysuckle
and salt, and the flush-colored azaleas
in your fist were destined
for that little glass vase
on the windowsill,
where all the sunlight
looked like fairy-dust?

what if infinity lived in a ride
upon your father's shoulders,
back when you were still little enough to carry?
back when you still believed in flying?
remember the way he held you there?
remember how it was as though
the world had expanded?
like you could see everything?
like you could see the end of the sky?

what if eternity didn't have to last
forever? what if it existed in a moment,
a memory, and then it drifted off
into the ether? what if heaven
was happening
right now?

to write

to write is to tunnel headfirst into difficult truths. with these cyclone minds we burrow into blank pages, down, down, until we reach magma. until we reach the core of emotion and clutch it for ourselves, let our eyes feast upon the heart of all love, all pain, all chest-clenching and cheek-warming. to write is to sense that your lungs are brimming with ink. it is to let that ink crawl up your throat and onto the paper like sweet-fire bile, the elixir of both honesty and falsehood. to write is to harness the ink that was choking you, drowning you, and reshape into words. it is to scrawl your pain and pleasure across the walls. to write is to love and hate and hurt all at once without being able to tell which feeling is which.

to read

to read is to wander into a dark forest—one that smells of wet earth and feels like folklore—with all intentions of getting lost. go, now. let your brain fade. float into the unknown. duck between branches and dart between shrubs and befriend every fox you encounter as you stroll deeper, deeper into the foliage. to read is to walk through an ivory fog and see a world that's cloaked in clouds. and yes, there will be moments when the ground beneath you falls away and you see only shadows, endings, the deaths of friends who never existed beyond these woods, these pages. but there will always be a new story. there will always be another forest. to read is to know that there are millions of dreamlands out there, waiting patiently for you to drift into them.

sweetening

when your past is not pretty enough
for your audience to swallow, coat
each story in syrup. a spoonful of sugar

helps the broken glass go down, so soften
the stab of your memories with laughter.
convince them that what doesn't kill you

makes you funnier. clasp the truth
in one hand and a fistful of sandpaper
in the other and file away

at history's jagged edges
until the unsavory pieces fall away.
water down the acid of your autobiography

until it goes down easy. until the poison
tastes like an antidote.

the body i'm in
(inspired by God Must Hate Me *by Catie Turner)*

hello up there, it's me again,
trying to appeal to a ceiling
that may be just a ceiling
but i'd like to believe is you.
all i'm asking for are reasons.
did your hands slip? were you
looking for a laugh? an earthly
freakshow for you and the angels
to chuckle at from above?
i'll admit, i don't know the etiquette
when it comes to this whole praying thing,
but shouldn't we, your fallible creations,
your defective designs, have a right
to be angry? aren't we allowed
to be furious with you for crafting
these dungeons of damaged skin
we're trapped in?
i don't mean to sound bitter.
i'm sure there's a proverb that explains
why i'm not allowed to know the answers
to these questions, but i'm too tired
to go about discovering it. instead
i'll keep arguing with the ceiling
that may be just a ceiling,
but i'd like to believe
is you.

the wrecked leading the wrecked

we had matching damage,
you always said. it was true
and it was cruel. you and me
and our identical fractures
were fixated on fixing each other,
like totaled cars acting as tow-trucks.
how could we have known
that we were silently self-destructing
every time we tried to close up
each other's cracks
with cement scraped from our own?
we were neck-deep in the same quicksand,
fighting to hoist one another
out of harm's way, and only
propelling ourselves down deeper,
deeper, into the sludge.

my fault lines have scarred over now,
and i don't know you anymore.
in leaving, we have saved ourselves
in the same way we once thought
we could save each other.

we were magic, and we were mythic,
and we were always
going to end up
poisoning each other.

The Mental Hospital Type

"You don't look like the mental hospital
type," she said,
her eyes traveling up and down
my body, as if trying to pick out
the exact molecule that turned me crazy.
"No offense," she said. "I just don't see it."
I wanted to say,
"Are you expecting me to give you a
guided tour of the most morbid corners
of my mind?"
I wanted to say,
"Here, come to the psychiatrist's office
with me, we'll have a group discussion."
I wanted to say,
"Choose whichever molecule you please.
They've all been corrupted. By now,
they're all crazy, every last cell."
But instead I just smiled and said,
"It wasn't that bad."
And she said, "So why'd you go?"
And I said, "It wasn't my choice."
And she said, "Shit. Did you, like,
break the law? Kidnap someone?"
I thought it was strange that *that* was where
her mind went, but I didn't say it out loud.
I also didn't tell her about
how my heart used to rattle

69

like busted machinery. How it creaked,
whimpered, like a lion
jammed into a birdcage. Instead I said,
"My parents thought it'd be best."
And she said, "You're being vague."
And I said, "That's true."
And it was true, because craziness
and vagueness go palm in weary palm.
Because sinking is something to be kept
at a whisper. Because no matter how loud
your wordless words are wailing,
they are still secrets, and you still
aren't saying them.

here lies

how peculiar is it to mourn
what was never yours.
the almost-people, the gravestones
with uncapitalized inscriptions.
how inelegant it is to move on
from something that never was.
something that we cannot name.
a spark that the kindling rejected
as unworthy of a flame. the vows
all got stuck in our windpipes,
replaced only by wrinkled-bedsheet
treaties of *we-are-nearly-something*
and *we-will-soon-be-nothing.*
like playing house
in a burning building, you told me.
i wish we had a name
for what we're burying,
like lover or stranger
or even friend, but the fog
we hid out fledgling bodies in
is still too thick to see through.

above ground

the beautiful thing about feeling
so small that you're sure
you could drift off with the dandelions
and no one would know but the wind
is the stillness afterward
in which you realize
that you're still there.
you're still there.
because it seems like the world
is going to swallow you
until it doesn't. *it doesn't.*
it simply accepts your matter,
and you do not get sucked down
into the dirt, and you are not
absorbed by the swamp of society,
and no one asks questions, and no one
has answers, because all that matters,
is that your feet are atop
this glorious surface and your head
is still above the boneyard.
you, rare creature, are still a fragment
of the earth, small and spartan
and surrounded by miracles.

untapped

it is a special kind of shame to burn out.
you must then carry your young self
around on your shoulders
for the rest of your days
and tremble under the weight of your own
expired potential. and you'll know
all the while that you are doomed
to eventually drop this stranger-of-a-child
who has not yet learned the half-hearted
art of being a let down. the child—
the dreamer you used to be—
who knows nothing of the mundane
monstrosities we call the real world.
where did all your promise go to die?
they'll ask once your excellence
turns into exhaustion.
and you'll think, *you're wrong.*
it isn't dead. i let it go free. i let my young self
fly away to a better place. maybe heaven,
or maybe a quiet little playground full of daisies
and wild things and youth without the risk
of aging. maybe that's where my promise
went to live.

limbo

she liked the phrase "in limbo."

she'd always been good at those birthday party
games in which an overwhelmed parent would hold
out a stick, and a line of sweaty children would proceed
to contort themselves in ungodly ways to try and fit
underneath it. there was no better feeling than emerging
from beneath the boundary untouched and being
crowned the limbo champion, candy-stickied fists
raised towards the streamers in triumph.

it was fitting, perhaps, that she'd go on to spend her
later years playing and replaying that very same game.
she made a sport of ducking underneath bottom lines.
pushing breaking points. making herself as small as
possible in a futile attempt to win an un-winnable
game.

*limbo. [lim·bo]. noun. 1. a transitional place, a state of
being between life and death.*

but it wasn't really life and death for her, was it? it
was more like life and being *alive.* still, that gap, the one
that set inhaling apart from breathing, looking apart
from seeing, seemed too abstract to even begin to
understand. the space between life and death—some
inconsequential number of heartbeats—was far more

defined.

defined enough, at least, to be able to test the limits of.

tell me you would stay

if a red flag was strung
in the middle of the sea,
with no one there to see it,
no one but me,
if my boat sprung a leak,
if my flares went unseen,
would the sunken ship ever be found?

if the earth opened up
like the mouth of a liar,
and i stood on the edge,
a friend of the fire,
if the void called my name,
if i sunk to get higher,
would there be peace
underneath the ground?

if i found myself lost
in a wasteland of grey,
and the words in my throat
were too stale to say,
if i sealed my lips shut,
didn't speak one more day,
would my silence make a sound?

if the rot in my roots
were to spread to my heart,

and all that was left
was my flesh and my art,
if my smile and my soul
began drifting apart,
could i rest for these next few rounds?

if you'd whisper a tale
to these old spare parts,
i could rest for these next few rounds.

what will last

i do not know very much for certain,
but i know that there is more
for you to be in this life than a body.
this skin we're in won't last,
and i assure you, the undertaker
will pay no mind to the shape
of your hips.

once we're gone there is nothing
left for our bodies to do
but shrivel. i see no point
in doing that same shriveling
while we're still around, too.

what will last are the memories,
the stories, the art. what will last
are the tales of triumph and tragedy,
the beauty of a imperfect object,
the quiet joy of a good friend.

we really don't have so long
to live these moments, these small
forevers. why waste such a rare
thing as life on a such a flimsy
thing as a body? you have so much
more to be than that.

you are the closest i get

will you stay even if i never
learn how to trust? will you
still lie beside me if this armor
turns out just to be my skin?
please understand that i can't risk
baring my soul to you;
it's a bad patch job of sharp corners
and i won't be the reason you bleed.
no amount of love will be enough
for me to reveal my weak spots,
my raw nerves, to you
or to anyone. i adore you,
but i will not show you how to hurt me.
please know that if i were to believe
in anyone, it would be in you.
but all of my wires are crossed,
my dear, and all of my Achilles' heels
are buried too far underground
for even the tree roots to touch.

graduation

my childhood bed doesn't smell the same,
and my stuffed animals
 haven't been told goodnight
in far too long, and my dog must not
understand why i'm not around anymore.
before i flung my cap and gown
and cautions to the wind,
i had a destination: *out.*
i made every moment into nothing more
than a stepping stone for my departure—
the linoleum glory of high school
became an empty catalyst for the wonders
that i assumed lay beyond it.
maybe i only latched so tightly
onto the idea of escaping because i knew
i had to leave. time wasn't going to wait
up for me—the hands of the clock
were shoving me forwards, so i handcrafted
a fantasy of an adventurer forging ahead
into the beautiful unknown.
a longing-less soul who had no need
to pine for the bright-eyed naivety
of not knowing anything at all.
but now i'm back in my childhood bed,
the one that smells like it belongs
to someone else, and i leave again
tomorrow, and my dog will once again

be left to wonder where i've gone.
if i was strong enough to stave off
the clock's hands, maybe even
to drive them backwards,
i'd make those years mean something
more than leaving.
i'd make myself see that precious time.
 as a gift rather than an escape route.
in the rear-view mirror,
life seems so much shorter.

flip-side

if the sirens sang lullabies
they would sound like eulogies
for all of the people
i never became. visions
of inverted lives
soothe me to sleep each night.
i gulp down opposite existences
like capsules of melatonin.
we all want what we can't
decipher.
what is doom
if not the thought
of being stuck with ourselves?

lightning bug lover

if i could wander back to the wilder days,
i'd capture all the fire
in the look on your face.
i'd seal it in a jar so it would never fly away.
my lightning bug lover,
this time i'd be good enough to stay.

if i could catch a spark
in the cup of my palm,
i'd shield your precious light
from the things i've done wrong.
i'd pick you every dandelion,
sing you every song.
my lightning bug lover,
this time i would learn how to be strong.

so know that if you ever long
to flicker back this way
my lightning bug lover,
this time i'd be good enough to stay.

trigger finger

the bullet you fired at me—
point-blank, with your hand
on my cheek—when you said
i was too much—*too, i don't know,*
dark and stormy and, like, heavy.
everything you say is just heavy
and i really can't deal with it anymore—
is still stuck somewhere
underneath my skin.
the entrance wound is an abyss
that takes up my entire skeleton.
there is no exit wound.
no relief from your memory.
i still cannot extract
your lead-heavy scorn.
you have tattered my spirit.
you have turned me into a ghost-girl
made from a bedsheet
full of holes.

ring around the rosie

ring around the rosie
she loves him but she knows he
lives in flashes
like an ever-hidden frown

ring around the rosie
she marvels at the rose he
sharpens, slashes
across her evening gown

ring around the rosie
she'll hold him even though he
claws and crashes
her spirit to the ground

ring around the rosie
he scares her so he knows she
won't dare smash his
counterfeited crown

ashes, ashes
he strikes her down

the secret-keeper

i'll play the role of a captive priest
in a confessional booth,
shackled to the far side of the curtain
as you spew your shame.
i'll recite my lines—
it wasn't your fault, you are forgiven—
with ease, mechanical ease, like the words
are wrenching their way up from my gut.
i'll store your secrets, be your mouthpiece
for empty absolution, just a vessel
who nods along to your soft-spoken lies.
i'll make myself into a lost-and-found box,
sweeping up your leftover heartaches,
collecting all the skeletons you can't fit
in your own closet.
i'll let you hook your anchor
onto the sunken remains of my ship
so that my ruins may keep you moored down.
so that my debris becomes your foothold.
step on my shoulders to hoist yourself higher.
gather up my embers
to build yourself a brighter fire.
sometimes i think
i was made to be a silo
for your scraps.

last times

the impossible thing about last times
is that all too often, they slip by unnoticed,
like a precious jewel through a storm drain.
how can we be sure which time
will be the last?
how do we know which goodbyes
are truly endings?

oftentimes, as a child,
i mistook dragonflies for fairies,
but i cannot seem to recall the last instance
in which i saw an angel in an insect.
i suppose it's because every moment
of false magic was just as wonderful
and indiscernible as the last.
and i wonder, the very last tooth i lost,
was it a molar or a canine?
what was the last word of the last book
my mother read aloud to me?
when did you last hold my cheeks
in your hands?

if i had known such lovely customs
would never occur again,
i would've stared harder
at that last dragonfly,
studied the last tooth,

held onto the last word,
memorized the feeling
of your palms on my face.
i would've memorized it all.
but the cracks in my consciousness
have swallowed up my pictures of the past,
and all i am left with is a collection
of unfinished stories.
of jewels drowned in sewers.
of forgotten last times.

up to you

at the edge of the world there is quiet.
everyone who has stood on the brink
of nothingness, like a bird stalled in the sky,
knows that when you are balancing
atop the banister that separates leaving
from staying, the only whisper of noise
is your heart puttering on,
its steady *thud-thud* asking you
whether or not
you would like the quiet
to trade places
with silence.

random word generator poem #3: oak, moon, belly, temple

after "The Two-Headed Calf " by Laura Gilpin

nestled in the belly of the rotting oak tree,
a barn owl and her babies
lie huddled together. the mother,
with her chamomile yellow eyes

and quick-snap wings, does not know
that come tomorrow, when the moon
fades off into the baby blue pallor
of the daytime sky,

men with hardhats and chainsaws
are coming to tear this sickly tree—
riddled with fungus and mildew,
half-crumbled, termite-chewed—

limb from limb. but tonight,
the barn owl sits in her moss-eaten temple
without worry of extermination.
tonight, her children are fed
and they've nuzzled up beside her
and there, in the hollow trunk
of that doomed oak tree,
she understands
that she is home.

morning oath

the sun has not yet scaled the sky
but i have already memorized

the topography of your goosebumps. you
always say you wish you could give me

gold necklaces and silk linens, but we are
far more beautiful here, on these worn cotton

sheets, free from the weight of jewels.
i don't want the moon. i want just you

and all of your forevers. i want to watch
you sleep underneath the carnelian light

of dawn spilling over into day. i want
to watch you wake, watch you come to life

like a cowboy in a toy box rouses
when the children leave the room.

questions for the cosmos

if it were up to me, we'd all build
shrines to stardust.
we'd worship celestial confetti
and pray to dark matter,
to the god of the void. i want to stare
into eclipses and let them burn
my eyes, let their glory
be branded into my skin.
i want to name gravity a sin.
maybe then i'll be weightless enough
to kneel at the altar of a silver-skinned deity
and tell the moon how much i adore her.
someone take me to a church
above the atmosphere so i can ask the cosmos
all of the impossible questions
that have built up in my brain like plaque
in an artery. are really alone down here?
are there beasts like us a few galaxies over?
do the supernovas hurts when they burn?
do the stars write wills?
do they bid their friends goodbye?
when they flare up and detonate,
those bombs made out of angel tears,
who grieves for the forgotten suns?

burial

some days, all you can do
is pay a visit to the graveyard
of your past selves and lay flowers
on their tombstones. share air
with their ghosts. tell them
you have not forgotten
the way they used to sketch the sky
as one great blue line. tell them
you've kept their memories safe,
kept their dreams in mind.
spend a little while lying in that cemetery
full of your dearly departed identities,
staring up at the sun
that you once drew as a yellow arc
in the corner of the page.

reasons to stay

I. for all the friends you haven't met yet. for the twinkling sound of their laughter. for their dreams. for the way they listen to yours. for the contented hush of the moments you spend side-by-side, hand-in-hand, not saying anything at all.

II. for all the books you haven't read yet. for their crisp, creamy pages, their woodland smell. for the fantasy worlds that you have not yet visited, the characters that you have not traded secrets with. for the happily-ever-afters and the teardrop-spattered the-ends. for what a wondrous thing it is to feel so much because of paper and ink.

III. for all the animals you haven't pet yet. for the way they sink into your touch. for confidence with which they know, regardless of words, without a common language, that you are a friend.

IV. for all the nooks of nature that you haven't seen yet. for the lily pads and white-speckled fawns and great green meadows. for the sun and the rain and the snow and the impossible way they each come down to greet us, come down to briefly hold our hands.

V. for the trillions of cells inside you. for their unwavering efforts to keep you going. for their strength, their might, their tiny little iron wills. stay because they're still fighting for you. stay so you can fight for them, too.

lava

in the playground days,
when we kneeled in sandboxes
that crusted out knees in grit and grime,
you and i, with our stubborn,
stubby hands, were determined to dig
all the way down to lava. we yearned to feel
the warmth of the red-hot ooze.
yearned to lay our eyes upon its brilliant color,
like a monarch butterfly set alight.

we didn't know back then
that even if we were mighty enough,
(tough enough, old enough)
to excavate that fiery fluid,
it would surely scorch our skin
to cinders.

i miss being able to dream dangerous
dreams and believe that they are wise.
i miss the sort of invincibility
that came with not knowing
the bounds of what was possible.

when i say words will never be enough

what i mean is that words are vast
and limitless and quite possibly all
that we have and they are not
nearly enough.

what i mean is that i can compare you
to every summer's day and snowy evening,
and the images will stretch far beyond
any heaven i'll ever brush fingertips with
on this earth and yet they will never reach
the end of the horizon.

what i mean is that i can cough up
my demons onto blank pages
for the rest of my years and squeeze out
every truth i've ever known
and i still will not have written
the story of my life.

what i mean is that even when
i am laid to rest, there will be
conversations left unfinished.
words left sitting unsaid
on my cold, quiet lips.

what i mean is that even
the loose-leaf offerings

the poets toss up towards the clouds,
these paper airplanes full of soul,
will one day drift back down to land.

and still, we dream.
still, we fling our postcards of prose
towards the heavens, and hope
that the sky will one day
throw an ink-stained airplane
of its own wonderfully inadequate words
back down to us in reply.

if love lives by a lakeside

this is wonderland
and no one else is here to see it.
it's sunset, and the lake is a blushing mirror
of the cherry blossom sky. beyond the reeds,
among the lily pads, two swans
have laced their necks together
into a double helix.
i'm not sure exactly, what it means
to be a soulmate, but i do know
that that's love, right there,
that tangle of feather and feeling.

what a crime it is,
that this evening will leave
no trace behind
once the night trickles off
into the backlog of time.

the healing logs

i am not going to tell you about the
shattering, because really,
it's the least interesting part.
yes, there were abysses and
aching bones and a few bleak fantasies
involving funerals, but i have spat out
those stories so many times
to faceless white coats with notepads
that they've begun to taste like decay
on my tongue. i contain storage lockers
of moth-eaten memories, libraries
of redundant sorrow.
i will not bore you
with these bygone diaries.
they are layered with dust for a reason.

but the picking up the pieces,
the elmer's glue and elbow grease
i used to patchwork my scraps
back together, i refuse to let those pages
yellow. i will tell and retell the stories
of my mending because to let those
volumes collect dust would be to let the
ashes outweigh the phoenix.

remember your rising.
restate it until it hurts.

the caving in will teach you
how to drag yourself upright.
but the reconstructing will show you
how to build a better ground.

wish come true

i regret the eyelashes i spent
wishing for impossible things
like endlessness. all of the coins
i wasted pleading for immortality.
every shooting star i begged
to make me indestructible.
i no longer need to be bulletproof.
infinity sounds exhausting, anyway.
just let the dandelions grant me
rich days and mellow nights.
all i require is one soft, gentle lifetime.

the driftwood people

the driftwood people meet up by the coast,
where family looks like debris.
when everyone's damaged, no one is lost,
and rubble makes good company.

us driftwood folk, we don't ask for much,
just that you know we were here.
long ago, we were forests
with so much to lose,
now we're fragments with nothing to fear.

so we'll let ourselves float,
resign to the tides,
tell the gods they can keep all their grace.
and we'll build us a home
made of wreckage and rain
where broken-down wonders take place.

we won't sweep up the pieces,
won't un-break the glass,
won't pin up our cheeks into smiles.
we'll cry and we'll scream
and we'll bask in our grief
and we'll stack up our driftwood in piles.

for the honor of pain, for the dawn of relief,
we'll stack up our driftwood in piles.

for everyone staying afloat

for those whose smiles
are tricks of the light,
and for those who believe
that each flicker of light
is just another fire waiting to die
and bleed smoke into their eyes.
for those who have grown up
grabbing at fistfuls of smoke
in hopes of preventing its departure,
and for those whose fists
slip through drywall when their voices
get stuck in their stomachs.
for those who stomachs are twisted
into sailor's knots, and for those who sail
through puddles expecting to cross oceans,
and for those who have surrendered
to the ocean, to the vicious cycle
 of the tides, to giving and the taking
and then giving a little more.
to letting the waves crash
and allowing the sand
to grind beneath their teeth
and giving in to the fact that the water
has never stopped rising,
and that no amount of life-vests
in the world will quell
the clamor of the sea.

* * *

for those who cannot make peace
with the clock
and for those who cannot
turn it backwards;
i wish you a million good days.
i wish you a lifetime.

fusion

statistically, at some point or another,
our hearts will beat
at exactly the same time.

you and i, sweet stranger,
will feel the same thrum

of life and all its wonders, of wildflowers
and summer dew and the smell of the sea.

there are so many earthly marvels
to stay for, but if you find yourself
running out of reasons,

please know that i am so looking forward
to the moment when our pulses
thud in harmony.

and after our rhythm falls again out of sync,
i will be waiting,
like the moon for the nightfall,

for the next time we align.

dear fellow accidental grown-ups

welcome to the in-between.
we live in a half-grown state of limbo.
i wish i could tell you
that i've discovered how to rewind,
retrace my own timeline and sneak
back, unseen, into childhood,
but it appears we're stuck here
in this waiting room of time.
mortality is such a strange beast.
stranger still is our position relative to it.
here we are in no-man's land,
the middle of the road,
staring out at the storm-purple horizon,
wondering whether the tornado
is traveling towards or away from us.
but it's really not so bad up here
on this ridge between birth and death,
the two great two chasms of shadows.
come now, dear friend.
wander the in-between with me.

i'll show you
    what it means
        to toe the line.

eliza grant

Find me on social media!

TikTok:
@wordwillneverbeenough
Instagram:
@words.will.never.be.enough
Email:
wordswillneverbeenough@gmail.com

Author's Note

I have always been captivated by the transference of words to a page. I consider language to be my greatest love affair. And yet, it is also language that frightens me more than anything else. There are limitless configurations of words, infinite ways to express the same feeling, but at the same time, it often feels quite impossible to pin a feeling down exactly, to describe an emotion or moment so perfectly that it rings true. Incontrovertibly *true*. And then, of course there's the ever-present question of time. How much time will I receive in this lifetime to put all the thoughts in my head into writing? How many words will I get? Which ones, if any, will stick?

I would like to thank all of you for allowing my words to mean something. Without readers, there are no writers. I am constantly astounded by the fact that there are people out there who care about what I have to say.

Thank you a million times. Thank you for everything.

tell the fireflies i'm sorry

eliza grant

Made in the USA
Coppell, TX
25 March 2022

75520951R00069